Learn to C

D0327583

Learn the basics of crochet with right and left-hand diagrams while making a coaster. Then practice your new skillswithfiv e more easy projects. Free online technique videos are available as a bonus tool!

LOOK FOR THE CAMERA in our instructions and watch our bonus technique videos made just for you! **www.LeisureArts.com/75491**

LEISURE ARTS, INC.
Maumelle, Arkansas

Learn to crochet your first project!

Coaster

This coaster is just right for learning the basics of crochet.
You can complete one in just an hour or so!

First, gather the supplies you will need!

Take a look at the Shopping List below. You only need 3 things to make each coaster.

SHOPPING LIST

Yarn
(Medium Weight Cotton) 🧶 **MEDIUM 4**
- ☐ 25 yards (23 meters) **each**

Crochet Hook
- ☐ Size H (5 mm)

Additional Supplies
- ☐ Yarn needle for hiding yarn ends

1. Yarn — You will need a medium weight yarn 🧶 **MEDIUM 4** for the Coaster. When buying yarn, look on the yarn label for the icon given in your shopping list 🧶 **MEDIUM 4**. A cotton yarn will give the best result for your coaster, as cotton absorbs moisture. Choose a light or bright color so it will be easier to see your stitches while you are learning.

2. Crochet Hook — Hooks come in different sizes and materials. You'll find them typically made from metal, plastic, wood, or bamboo. For this project, use a size H (5 mm).

3. Yarn Needle — A yarn needle is typically made from plastic or metal and will have a large eye and a blunt tip. It is used to weave the yarn ends into the Coaster to hide them.

Now, you're ready to start!

The diagrams for learning the basic stitches and a few other techniques are shown in right and left-handed versions. Some diagrams have shaded areas on the yarn. This is intended to specify the technique being referenced in the diagram.

▓ To make a slip knot, pull a length of yarn from the skein. Make a circle on top of the yarn that comes from the skein about 6" (15 cm) from the end *(Fig. 1a)*.

Fig. 1a

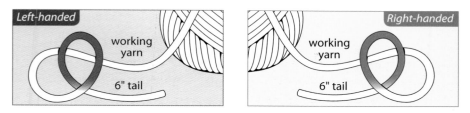

Slip your hook under the strand in the middle of the circle *(Fig. 1b)*.

Fig. 1b

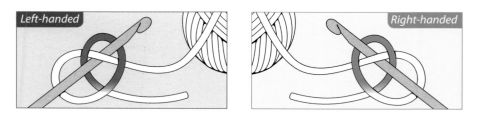

Pull on both strands to tighten the slip knot *(Fig. 1c)*.

Fig. 1c

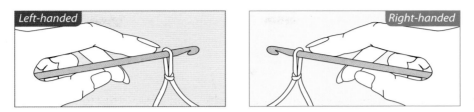

Pull the working yarn to tighten the loop around the **working area** of your hook until it fits closely but slides easily *(Fig. 1d)*.

Fig. 1d

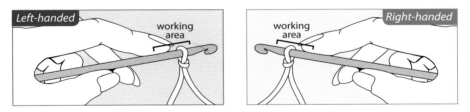

TIP The great thing about the slip knot is that it's easy to adjust and also to un-do. To practice, just slip the hook out of the loop and pull on both ends of the yarn until the slip knot disappears!

Hold your hook like a table knife in your dominant hand *(Fig. 2)*.

Fig. 2

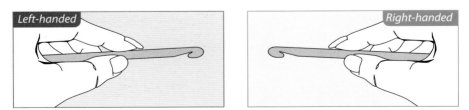

Hold your yarn by laying the working yarn over the index finger of your other hand. Hold the slip knot with your thumb and middle finger of that hand (to keep the slip knot from moving) and fold your other fingers over the yarn in your palm *(Fig. 3)*.

Fig. 3

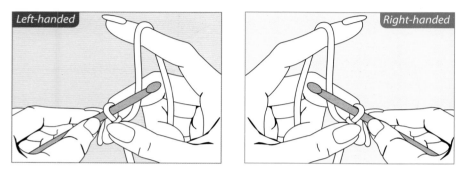

 To make a chain, begin with the slip knot on your hook.

TIP *A "yarn over" is the process of placing the yarn over your hook* and is used in every stitch you will learn.

First, Yarn Over, placing the yarn **behind** your hook and **over the top** *(Fig. 4a)*.

Fig. 4a

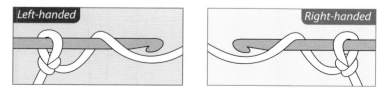

Next, to complete the chain, turn the tip of your hook toward you and slide your hook toward the loop on your hook, catching the yarn with the tip *(Fig. 4b)*, then point the tip of your hook down (so it won't get caught on the side of the loop) as you draw the yarn through the loop on your hook *(Fig. 4c)* forming a new loop. Slide the new loop onto the working area of the hook. The chain just made is below the loop on your hook *(Fig. 4d)*.

Fig. 4b

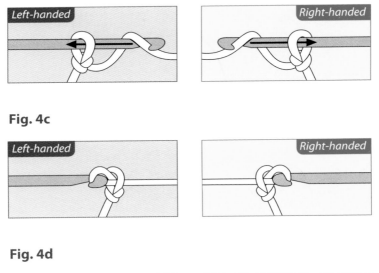

Fig. 4c

Fig. 4d

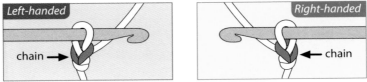

Make sure the loop fits closely around the working area of your hook and that the chain is the size of the hook.

Follow the steps in **Figs. 4a-d** to make 5 more chains.

TIP

To make the chains even and the correct size, it's important to allow the yarn to move smoothly through your fingers.

Look at your chain; the **front** of the chain looks like
a series of V's *(Fig. 5a)*.

Fig. 5a

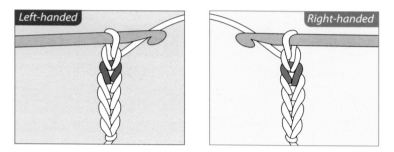

The **back** of the chain has a ridge behind each chain stitch *(Fig. 5b)*.

Fig. 5b

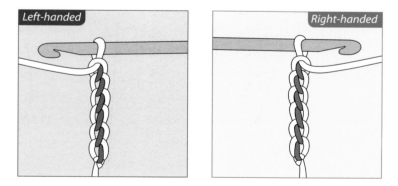

Count your chains starting at the first chain **after** the loop on your hook and count back to the slip knot *(Fig. 6)*. You should have 6 chains.

Fig. 6

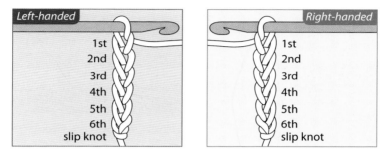

 If your hook slips out of a stitch, reinsert it through the **front** of the stitch without twisting the loop *(Fig. 7)*.

Fig. 7

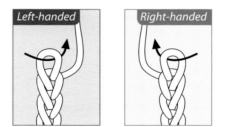

Coaster: Make 8 more chains to form the foundation, referred to as the beginning chain, for a total of 14 chains.

 TIP

Move your thumb and middle finger closer to the hook, as the chain grows longer, to keep control of the chain *(Fig. 8)*.

Fig. 8

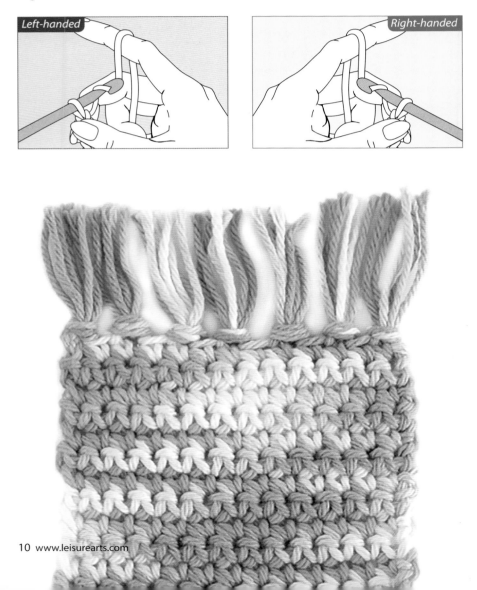

ROW 1

🎥 To work a single crochet in a chain, begin in the second
chain from your hook. Insert your hook under the **back ridge** of the
chain as indicated by the arrow *(Fig. 9a)*.

Fig. 9a

Yarn over, bringing the working yarn **behind** your hook and **over**
the top *(Fig. 9b)*.

Fig. 9b

Draw your hook back through the stitch, **pulling up a loop** *(Fig. 9c)*.

Fig. 9c

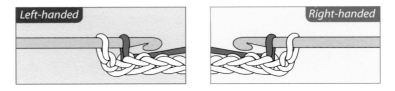

Yarn over (bringing the working yarn **behind** your hook and **over** the top) and draw the hook through both loops on your hook *(Fig. 9d)*, completing your first single crochet *(Fig. 9e)*.

Fig. 9d

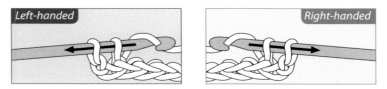

Fig. 9e

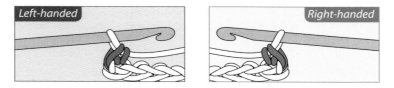

To make the next single crochet, insert your hook under the back ridge of the next chain and follow the steps in **Figs. 9b-e**, page 11.

Continue to work a single crochet in each chain across the beginning chain, for a total of 13 single crochets *(Photo A)*.

Photo A

Count your stitches at the end of each row. Each stitch will have a V-shape at the top, just as the front of your chain did *(Fig. 10)*.

Fig. 10

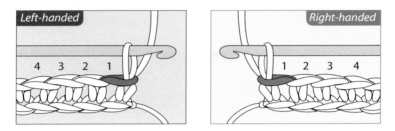

ROW 2

Chain 1 (to raise the yarn to the height of a single crochet), then turn your work around *(Fig. 11a)*.

Fig. 11a

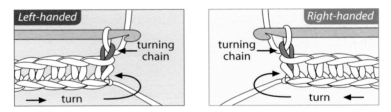

Working **under both top loops** of each single crochet, insert your hook in the first single crochet (closest to the hook) *(Fig. 11b)*, following the steps in **Figs. 9b-e**, page 11, work a single crochet in each single crochet across.

Fig. 11b

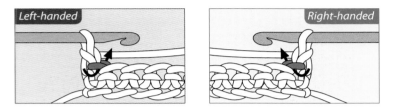

Make sure you work in the last stitch of the row *(Fig. 11c)*. You will have 13 single crochets. Count your stitches.

Fig. 11c

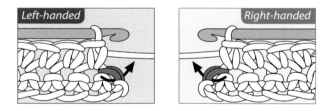

TIP It's okay if your Coaster isn't perfect. However, if at any time you are not happy with your work, or you've made a mistake and would like to correct it, you can. Remove your hook from the loop and pull on the working yarn until you have ripped back to the mistake. Then insert the hook back into the loop *(Fig. 7, page 9)*.

ROWS 3-14

Work same as Row 2. Count your stitches at the end of each row to make sure you have 13 single crochets.

Count the rows to make sure you have 14. The front of a single crochet (Rows 1 & 3) has 2 vertical legs and the back (Row 2) has a horizontal bar *(Fig. 12)*.

Fig. 12

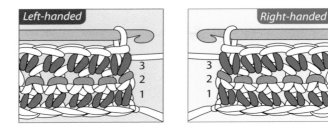

Good Job!

You completed the basic square of your Coaster. Now choose what type of finishing you want to use on the edges.

FINISHING

Putting Fringe on the ends (Photo B) is one of the easiest finishing techniques; see page 16 for instructions. For a more tailored edge, try the Slip Stitch Edging all around the piece (Photo C); learn how on page 17.

Photo B - Fringe

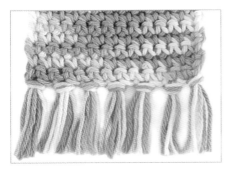

Photo C - Slip Stitch Edging

COASTER WITH FRINGE

To finish off, cut the yarn leaving a 6" (15 cm) end. Remove the loop from your hook and bring the end through the last loop, pulling the end to tighten it *(Fig. 13)*.

Fig. 13

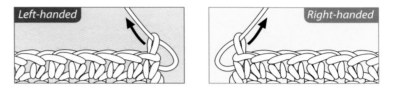

At this point, the Coaster doesn't have a right or wrong side. The knot formed on the fringe will be the right side *(see Photo B, page 15)*.

To make fringe, cut a piece of cardboard 3" (7.5 cm) square. Wind the yarn **loosely** and **evenly** around the cardboard 42 times, then cut across one end.

Add fringe across the last row and across the beginning chain, beginning in the first stitch then placing one in every other stitch across as follows: Hold 3 strands together and fold them in half. Using a crochet hook, draw the folded end up through a stitch on the Coaster and pull the loose ends through the folded end *(Fig. 14a)*; draw the knot up **tightly** *(Fig. 14b)*.

Lay the Coaster flat on a hard surface and trim the ends to 1¹/₂" (4 cm).

Fig. 14a

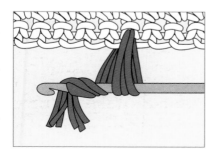

Fig. 14b

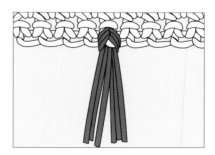

To weave in the yarn ends on the **wrong** side, thread a yarn needle with a yarn end, then insert the needle under the stitches, reversing the direction that you are weaving several times in the direction indicated by the arrow *(Fig. 15)*. Once the end is hidden, clip it close to the work. Repeat with the remaining yarn end.

Fig. 15

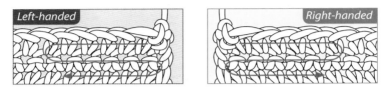

COASTER WITH SLIP STITCH EDGING

At this point, the Coaster doesn't have a right or wrong side. The side facing you as you work the Edging will become the **right** side.

Turn your work around.

To work a slip stitch, insert your hook in the first single crochet, yarn over (**behind** your hook and **over** the top) and draw your hook through the stitch **and** the loop on your hook *(Fig. 16a)*, completing the slip stitch *(Fig. 16b)*.

Fig. 16a

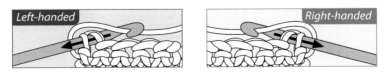

Fig. 16b

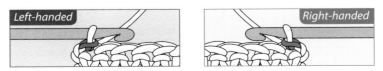

Working across the last row, chain 1, slip stitch in the next single crochet. Continue to chain 1, then work a slip stitch in the next single crochet across the row.

Begin working in the ends of the rows across the side of the Coaster, inserting your hook under 2 strands *(Fig. 17)*. Continue to chain 1, then work a slip stitch ▦ spacing them evenly to keep the Coaster laying flat.

Fig. 17

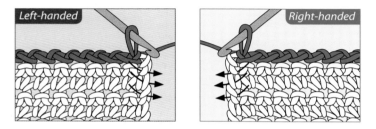

Begin working across the bottom of the beginning chain. Since you worked the first row of single crochets in the back ridge of the chains, the free loops look just like the top of stitches *(Fig. 18)*.

Fig. 18

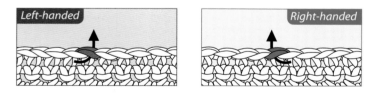

Continue to chain 1, then work a slip stitch across the bottom of the beginning chain and then evenly across the ends of the rows on the second side. End by working a chain 1.

To join the end of the round to the beginning of the round, slip st in the first slip stitch made at the beginning of the round *(Fig. 19)*.

Fig. 19

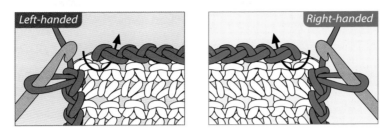

To finish off, cut the yarn leaving a 6" (15 cm) end. Remove the loop from your hook and bring the end through the last loop, pulling the end to tighten it *(Fig. 13, page 16)*.

To weave in the yarn ends on the **wrong** side, thread a yarn needle with a yarn end, then insert the needle under the stitches, reversing the direction that you are weaving several times in the direction indicated by the arrow *(Fig. 15, page 17)*. Once the end is hidden, clip it close to the work. Repeat with the remaining yarn end.

Congratulations!

You now know the basics of crochet AND have a Coaster to show off. To get comfortable with what you've learned, why not make a few more coasters and try following the condensed instructions on page 32? Pages 31-34 will help you learn how to read this abbreviated language.

When you're ready to learn some more new stitches, turn to the Spa Cloth on page 20.

Spa Cloth

Step up your learning with two new stitches that are progressively taller. Adding to the single crochets used in the Coaster, the Spa Cloth has half double crochets and double crochets. This versatile cloth makes a great gift along with luxurious soaps, or it can double as a dishcloth.

Finished Size: Approximately 10" (25.5 cm) square without edging

SHOPPING LIST

Yarn
(Medium Weight Cotton) 🧶**4**

[2 ounces, 95 yards (57 grams, 86 meters) per skein]:

☐ 1 skein

Crochet Hook
☐ Size H (5 mm)

Additional Supplies
☐ Marker - split ring or scrap yarn
☐ Yarn needle

STITCH GUIDE
🎥 Chain (*Figs. 4a-d, page 6*)
🎥 Back ridge of a chain and single crochet (*Figs. 9a-e, page 11*)
🎥 Slip stitch (*Figs. 16a & b, page 17*)

INSTRUCTIONS
Always begin with a slip knot on your hook. Chain 36 to start your Spa Cloth.

ROW 1
Working in the back ridge of the beginning chain, work a single crochet in the second chain from the hook and in each chain across: you will have 35 single crochets.

ROWS 2-5
Chain 1, turn your work; work a single crochet in each single crochet across: count your stitches to be sure you still have 35 single crochets.

ROW 6
This row is made up of half double crochets. A half double crochet begins with a yarn over that makes it taller than the single crochet.

Chain 2. **This will count as the first half double crochet.** Turn your work. Place a marker in the top of the turning chain-2 to mark it as the first stitch. This will help you identify the last stitch when working the next row. You can use a split ring marker *(Fig. 20a)* or a short piece of contrasting color yarn *(Fig. 20b)*. ***From here on, the marker is not shown in the drawings, so that you can see the stitches easier.***

Fig. 20a

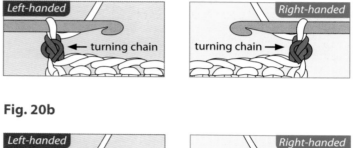

Fig. 20b

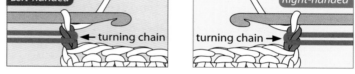

Since the turning chain-2 counts as a stitch, the first stitch of the previous row will not be worked into.

To work a half double crochet, begin in the **next** stitch. Yarn over (bringing the working yarn **behind** your hook and **over** the top), insert your hook under **both** top loops of the next stitch *(Fig. 21a)*.

Fig. 21a

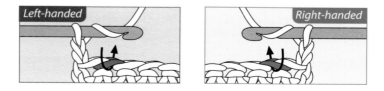

Yarn over (**behind** your hook and **over** the top) and draw your hook back through the stitch *(Fig. 21b)*, pulling up a loop. You will have 3 loops on your hook *(Fig. 21c)*.

Fig. 21b

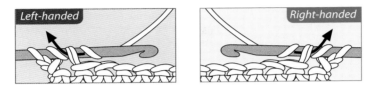

Fig. 21c

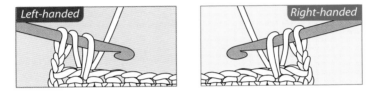

Yarn over and draw your hook through all 3 loops on your hook, completing the half double crochet *(Fig. 21d)*.

Fig. 21d

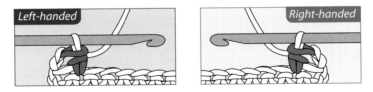

Following the steps in **Figs. 21a-d**, work a half double crochet in the **next** stitch and in each stitch across; at the end of the row, you will have 35 half double crochets including the turning chain-2.

ROW 7

Chain 2, place a marker in the top of the turning chain-2 (to mark it as the first stitch), turn your work. Work a half double crochet in the **next** stitch and in each stitch across including the marked turning chain-2 *(Fig. 22)*, remove the marker: 35 half double crochets.

Fig. 22

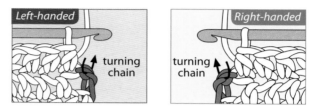

ROWS 8-10

Chain 2; turn your work. Continue to place a marker in the top of the turning chain-2 until you are confident where the last stitch is to be worked. Work a half double crochet in the **next** stitch and in each stitch across including the turning chain-2: 35 half double crochets.

ROW 11

This row is made up of double crochets. A double crochet starts the same as the half double crochet, but has one more step, making it a taller stitch.

Chain 3. **This will count as the first double crochet.** Turn your work *(Fig. 23)*. Place a marker in the top of the turning chain-3 to mark it as the first stitch.

Fig. 23

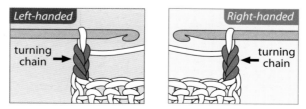

Since the turning chain-3 counts as a stitch, the first stitch of the previous row will not be worked into.

To work a double crochet, begin in the **next** stitch. Yarn over (bringing the working yarn **behind** your hook and **over** the top), insert your hook under **both** top loops of the next stitch *(Fig. 24a)*.

Fig. 24a

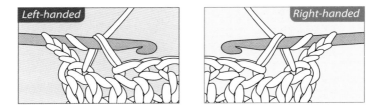

Yarn over and draw your hook back through the stitch *(Fig. 24b)*, pulling up a loop. You will have 3 loops on your hook *(Fig. 24c)*.

Fig. 24b

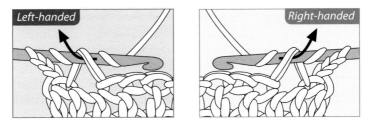

Fig. 24c

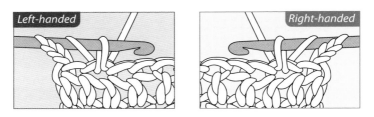

Yarn over and draw your hook through 2 loops on your hook *(Fig. 24d)*.

Fig. 24d

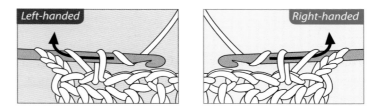

Yarn over again and draw through the remaining 2 loops on your hook *(Fig. 24e)*, completing the double crochet *(Fig. 24f)*.

Fig. 24e

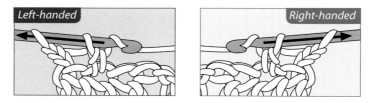

Fig. 24f

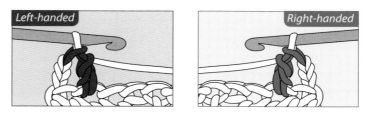

Following the steps in **Figs. 24a-f**, pages 25 and 26, work a double crochet in the next stitch and in each stitch across including the turning chain-2; at the end of the row, you will have 35 double crochets including the turning chain-3.

ROWS 12-15
Chain 3; turn your work. Continue to place a marker in the top of the turning chain-3 until you are confident where the last stitch is to be worked; work a double crochet in the **next** stitch and in each stitch across including the turning chain-3 *(Fig. 25)*: 35 double crochets.

Fig. 25

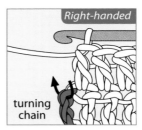

Photo D

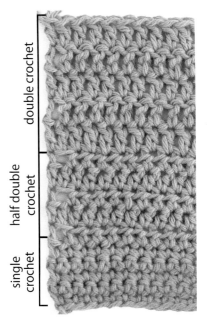

double crochet

half double crochet

single crochet

Stop and look at your work so far. Notice the height of the different stitches *(Photo D)*. Five rows have been worked in each stitch.

ROWS 16-20
Chain 2, turn your work; work a half double crochet in the **next** stitch and in each stitch across.

ROWS 21-25
Chain 1, turn your work; work a single crochet in each stitch across.

Congratulations!

Now you have expanded your stitch repertoire with half double crochet and double crochet stitches.

You can "finish off" *(Fig. 13, page 16)* your Spa Cloth and leave the edges plain *(Photo E)*, or add interest with the Scalloped Edging *(Photo F)*.

Photo E

Photo F - Scalloped Edging

SCALLOPED EDGING

Chain 1, turn your work.

🎥 **To work a V-Stitch** (and form a scallop), single crochet in the first single crochet, chain 2, work another single crochet all in the same stitch *(Fig. 26)*.

Fig. 26

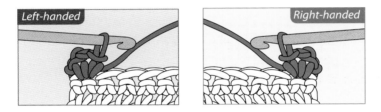

🎥 **To work a slip stitch**, insert your hook in the next single crochet, yarn over (**behind** your hook and **over** the top) and draw your hook through the stitch **and** the loop on your hook, completing the slip stitch *(Figs. 16a & b, page 17)*.

Work a V-stitch in the next single crochet.

Continue to work a slip stitch, then a V-stitch across the last row.

▶ Begin working in the ends of the rows across the side
of the Spa Cloth, inserting your hook under 2 strands *(Fig. 17, page 18)*.
Skip the first row and slip stitch in the next row.

Continue to work a V-stitch, then a slip stitch evenly across to keep the
Spa Cloth lying flat, ending by working a slip st.

Begin working in the free loops across the bottom of the
beginning chain. Since you worked the first row of single crochets in
the back ridges, the free loops look just like the top of stitches *(Fig. 18,
page 18)*.

Work across the bottom and the second side the same as you did for the
top and first side.

To join the end of the round to the beginning of the round,
insert your hook in the first single crochet made at the beginning of the
round *(Fig. 27)*, yarn over (bringing the working yarn **behind** your hook
and **over** the top) and draw your hook through the stitch **and** the loop
on your hook, completing the slip stitch.

Fig. 27

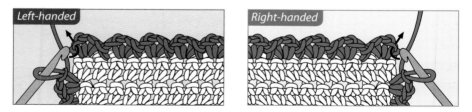

Finish off *(Fig. 13, page 16)*.

Weave in the yarn ends *(Fig. 15, page 17)*.

*You can make more spa cloths as you practice how to read a pattern,
page 32.*

How To Read A Pattern

When reading crochet instructions, read from punctuation mark to punctuation mark. As in grammar, commas (,) and semicolons (;) mean to pause and periods (.) mean stop.

Abbreviations

Crochet instructions are written in a condensed language consisting of abbreviations, punctuation marks, and other symbols. This saves time and space and is easy to read once you become familiar with it.

Here are the abbreviations used in this book.

ch(s)	chain(s)
cm	centimeters
dc	double crochet(s)
hdc	half double crochet(s)
mm	millimeters
sc	single crochet(s)
sp(s)	space(s)
st(s)	stitch(es)
YO	yarn over

To help you learn how to read typical crochet patterns, page 32 gives abbreviated versions of the Coaster and the Spa Cloth instructions. Try following these condensed patterns, and refer back to the teaching versions on pages 2 and 20 if you need help.

So that you can continue learning to read patterns, the Scarf on page 35 was written both with and without abbreviations.

Below is a chart listing crochet terms used in the United States and abroad.

CROCHET TERMINOLOGY		
UNITED STATES		INTERNATIONAL
slip stitch (slip st)	=	single crochet (sc)
single crochet (sc)	=	double crochet (dc)
half double crochet (hdc)	=	half treble crochet (htr)
double crochet (dc)	=	treble crochet(tr)
treble crochet (tr)	=	double treble crochet (dtr)
double treble crochet (dtr)	=	triple treble crochet (ttr)
triple treble crochet (tr tr)	=	quadruple treble crochet (qtr)
skip	=	miss

Coaster Instructions

Ch 14.

Row 1: Sc in back ridge of second ch from hook and in each ch across: 13 sc.

Rows 2-14: Ch 1, turn; sc in each sc across.

Finish off if you'd like to add fringe *(Figs. 14a & b, page 16)* instead of adding an edging.

EDGING

Turn; ★ (slip st in next st, ch 1) across; (slip st, ch 1) evenly across end of rows; repeat from ★ once **more**; join with slip st to first slip st, finish off.

Spa Cloth Instructions

Ch 36.

Row 1: Sc in back ridge of second ch from hook and in each ch across: 35 sc.

Rows 2-5: Ch 1, turn; sc in each sc across.

Rows 6-10: Ch 2 **(counts as first hdc)**, turn; hdc in next st and in each st across.

Rows 11-15: Ch 3 **(counts as first dc)**, turn; dc in next st and in each st across.

Rows 16-20: Ch 2 **(counts as first hdc)**, turn; hdc in next st and in each st across.

Rows 21-25: Ch 1, turn; sc in each st across.

Finish off or add the Scalloped Edging.

SCALLOPED EDGING
To work V-St, (sc, ch 2, sc) in st indicated.

Ch 1, turn; work V-St in first sc, (slip st in next sc, work V-St in next sc) across; working in end of rows, skip first row, slip st in next row, continue to work a V-St, then a slip st evenly across; working in free loops of beginning ch *(Fig. 18, page 18)*, work V-St in first ch, (slip st in next ch, work V-St in next ch) across; working in end of rows, skip first row, slip st in next row, continue to work a V-St, then a slip st evenly across; join with slip st to first sc, finish off.

Symbols in a Pattern

The numbers that you will find after a **colon (:)** are the number of completed stitches and/or spaces you should have at the end of the row you were working. This lets you know if you have worked the right number of stitches and/or spaces.

You will see instructions in this book that include **parentheses ( )** and **brackets [ ]**. They may contain explanatory remarks, such as the metric measurements after the finished sizes, or the meters of the yarn needed or an indication of the right side of a row.

Parentheses ( ) can also be used to indicate that several stitches are to be worked as a unit in the stitch or space indicated. For example, the V-Stitch is defined as, "(single crochet, chain 2, single crochet) in next stitch". All of the stitches inside the parentheses will be worked into the next stitch or space to form the V-Stitch.

Another use of parentheses is to indicate a repetition. The instructions inside the parentheses are worked across an edge. You can find an example of this in the Edging of the Coaster. "(slip st in next st, ch 1) across."

A star (★) is used to shorten instructions. Work all of the instructions following a ★ as many **more** times as indicated in addition to the first time.

The **skill levels** of patterns and the **yarn weights** are indicated by symbols, and can be found on the following charts.

Yarn Weight Symbol & Names	LACE (0)	SUPER FINE (1)	FINE (2)	LIGHT (3)	MEDIUM (4)	BULKY (5)	SUPER BULKY (6)
Type of Yarns in Category	Fingering, 10-count crochet thread	Sock, Fingering Baby	Sport, Baby	DK, Light Worsted	Worsted, Afghan, Aran	Chunky, Craft, Rug	Bulky, Roving
Crochet Gauge* Ranges in Single Crochet to 4" (10 cm)	32-42 double crochets**	21-32 sts	16-20 sts	12-17 sts	11-14 sts	8-11 sts	5-9 sts
Advised Hook Size Range	Steel*** 6,7,8 Regular hook B-1	B-1 to E-4	E-4 to 7	7 to I-9	I-9 to K-10.5	K-10.5 to M-13	M-13 and larger

*GUIDELINES ONLY: The chart above reflects the most commonly used gauges and hook sizes for specific yarn categories.

** Lace weight yarns are usually crocheted on larger-size hooks to create lacy openwork patterns. Accordingly, a gauge range is difficult to determine. Always follow the gauge stated in your pattern.

*** Steel crochet hooks are sized differently from regular hooks–the higher the number the smaller the hook, which is the reverse of regular hook sizing.

Gauge

Gauge is a term that refers to a measurement of stitches and rows in a specified area, and is especially important when making a project where fit is critical.

Since the projects in this book can be larger or smaller than the finished size without running out of yarn or being unusable, there are no gauges in the instructions for you to match.

Once your skills progress to the point you want to make a garment, gauge will become very important.

●□□□ BEGINNER	Projects for first-time crocheters using basic stitches. Minimal shaping.	
●■□□ EASY	Projects using yarn with basic stitches, repetitive stitch patterns, simple color changes, and simple shaping and finishing.	
●■■□ INTERMEDIATE	Projects using a variety of techniques, such as basic lace patterns or color patterns, mid-level shaping and finishing.	
●■■■ EXPERIENCED	Projects with intricate stitch patterns, techniques and dimension, such as non-repeating patterns, multi-color techniques, fine threads, small hooks, detailed shaping and refined finishing.	

CROCHET HOOKS															
U.S.	B-1	C-2	D-3	E-4	F-5	G-6	H-8	I-9	J-10	K-10½	L-11	M/N-13	N/P-15	P/Q	Q	S
Metric - mm	2.25	2.75	3.25	3.5	3.75	4	5	5.5	6	6.5	8	9	10	15	16	19

Remember, you can watch each technique online!
www.leisurearts.com/75491

Scarf

This design shows how stitches can be grouped to form a decorative pattern. The instructions are presented with and without abbreviations to help you continue learning how to read crochet patterns; choose the one you are most comfortable following. For a finishing touch, pom-pom instructions are also given.

■□□□▷ **BEGINNER +**

Finished Size: Approximately
5" x 70" (12.5 cm x 178 cm)

SHOPPING LIST

Yarn (Bulky Weight) 🧶**5**
[3 ounces, 144 yards
(85 grams, 13 meters)
per skein]:
☐ 2 skeins

Crochet Hook
☐ Size K (6.5 mm)

Additional Supplies
☐ Yarn needle

───── STITCH GUIDE ─────
🎥 Chain (*Figs. 4a-d, page 7*)
🎥 Back ridge of a chain (*Fig. 9a, page 11*)
🎥 Slip stitch (*Figs. 16a & b, page 17*)
🎥 Double crochet (*Figs. 24a-f, page 25*)

INSTRUCTIONS
with abbreviations
Ch 16.

Place a marker in the last ch made to mark the first dc on Row 1. Remove the marker after the ch is worked into.

Row 1 (Right side)**:** Working in back ridge of beginning ch, dc in fourth ch from hook **(3 skipped chs count as first dc)** and in each ch across: 14 dc.

Note: Loop a short piece of yarn around any stitch to mark Row 1 as **right** side.

A marker can also be placed in the top of the turning ch-3 of each row to mark it as the first dc, removing the marker after the stitch is worked into.

Row 2: Ch 3 **(counts as first dc, now and throughout)**, turn; 3 dc in next dc, ★ skip next 2 dc, 3 dc in next dc; repeat from ★ 2 times **more**, skip next 2 dc, dc in last dc (marked ch), remove marker: 4 groups of 3 dc and 1 dc on each end (14 dc).

Repeat Row 2 for pattern until Scarf measures approximately 69½" (176.5 cm) from beginning ch, ending by working a **wrong** side row.

Last Row: Ch 3, turn; dc in next dc and in each dc across; do **not** finish off.

Turn your work, then fold the last row in half with **right** side together. Working through **both** loops of **both** layers, slip st in first 7 dc to form a point *(Fig. 28, page 39)*; finish off.

Fold the first row in half with **right** side together. Working through free loops of beginning ch of **both** layers and beginning with a slip knot on your hook, slip st in first ch and in next 6 chs to form a point; finish off.

Turn points right side out *(Photo H, page 39)*.

Make two, 2" (5 cm) pom-poms *(Figs. 29a-c, page 39)*. Sew a pom-pom to the point at each end of the Scarf.

Weave in the yarn ends.

INSTRUCTIONS
without abbreviations
Chain 16 to start your scarf.

Place a marker in the first chain made to mark the last double crochet on Row 1. Remove the marker after the chain is worked into.

Instructions continued on page 38.

Row 1 (Right side)**:** Working in back ridge of beginning chain, work a double crochet in fourth chain from hook. The 3 skipped chains will count as the first double crochet on this row. Work a double crochet in the next 12 chains. You will have 14 double crochets.

Note: Loop a short piece of yarn around any stitch to mark Row 1 as **right** side.

A marker can also be placed in the top of the turning chain-3 of each row to mark it as the first double crochet, removing the marker after the stitch is worked into.

Row 2: Chain 3 (**counts as first double crochet, now and throughout**), turn; 3 double crochets in next double crochet, ★ skip next 2 double crochets, 3 double crochets in next double crochet; repeat from ★ 2 times **more**, skip next 2 double crochets, double crochet in last double crochet (marked turning chain), remove marker: 4 groups of 3 double crochets and 1 double crochet on each end.

Repeat Row 2 for pattern until Scarf measures approximately 69½" (176.5 cm) from beginning chain, ending by working a **wrong** side row.

Last Row: Chain 3, turn; double crochet in next double crochet and in each double crochet across; do **not** finish off.

Turn your work, then fold the last row in half with **right** side together. Working through **both** loops of **both** layers, slip stitch in first 7 double crochets to form a point *(Fig. 28)*; finish off.

Fold the first row in half with **right** side together. Working through free loops of beginning chain of **both** layers and beginning with a slip knot on your hook, slip stitch in first chain and in next 6 chains to form a point; finish off.

Turn points right side out *(Photo H)*.

Make two, 2" (5 cm) pom-poms *(Figs. 29a-c)*.
Sew a pom-pom to the point at each end of the Scarf.

Weave in the yarn ends.

Photo H   wrong side

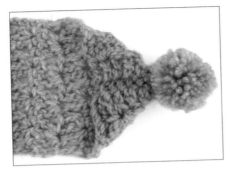

🎥 Slip Stitch Seams

With **right** side together and working through **both** loops of **both** layers, slip stitch across as indicated in instructions *(Fig. 28)*.

Fig. 28

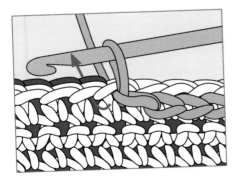

🎥 POM-POM

Cut a piece of cardboard 3" (7.5 cm) square. Wind the yarn around the cardboard until it is approximately ½" (12 mm) thick in the middle *(Fig. 29a)*.

Carefully slip the yarn off the cardboard and firmly tie an 18" (45.5 cm) length of yarn around the middle *(Fig. 29b)*. Leave yarn ends long enough to attach the pom-pom. Cut the loops on both ends and trim the pom-pom into a smooth ball *(Fig. 29c)*.

Fig. 29a

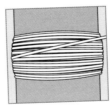

Fig. 29b

Fig. 29c

Hand Mitts

*These Hand Mitts are super easy
– there's no thumb to shape!
You simply leave an opening
for the thumb when you make
the seam. Other great features
are the mock ribbing and the
pretty pattern stitch.*

 **EASY**

Finished Size: Approximately 7" (18 cm) long with an adjustable width

STITCH GUIDE
Chain *(Figs. 4a-d, page 6)*
Back ridge of a chain and single crochet *(Figs. 9a-e, page 11)*
Slip stitch *(Figs. 16a & b, page 17)*
Double crochet *(Figs. 24a-f, page 26)*

INSTRUCTIONS
Ch 27.

Row 1 (Right side)**:** Working in back ridge of beginning ch, sc in second ch from hook and in next 3 chs, dc in next ch, ★ sc in next ch, dc in next ch; repeat from ★ across to last 5 chs, sc in last 5 chs: 26 sts.

Note: Loop a short piece of yarn around any stitch to mark Row 1 as **right** side.

The top and bottom of the Hand Mitt have a mock ribbing that is made by working sc in the Back Loops Only *(Fig. 30, page 47)*.

Row 2: Ch 1, turn; sc in Back Loop Only of first 4 sc, working in **both** loops, ★ dc in next sc, sc in next dc; repeat from ★ across to last 4 sc, sc in Back Loop Only of last 4 sc.

Repeat Row 2 for pattern until Hand Mitt measures approximately 7" (18 cm) from beginning ch **or** until desired width, ending by working a **wrong** side row; do **not** finish off.

Instructions continued on page 46.

HAND MITTS
Continued from page 45.

🎥 **To join the seam**, match the first and last rows with **right** sides together. Working through **both** loops of **both** layers *(Fig. 28, page 39)*, slip st in first 12 sts; working in front piece only, slip st in next 7 sts for thumb opening, working through **both** layers, slip st in last 7 sts; finish off.

Weave in the yarn ends.

COWL
Continued from page 41.

Repeat Row 2 for pattern until Cowl measures approximately 25" (63.5 cm) from beginning ch, ending by working a **wrong** side row; do **not** finish off.

🎥 **To join the seam**, match the first and last rows with **right** sides together. Working through **both** loops of **both** layers *(Fig. 28, page 39)*, slip st in each st across making sure the pattern lines up; finish off.

Weave in the yarn ends.

RIPPLE THROW
Continued from page 43.

📽 **To work in Back Loops Only,** work in loop indicated by arrow *(Fig. 30)*.

Fig. 30

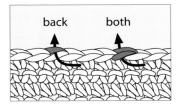

back   both

Row 2: Ch 3 **(counts as first dc),** turn; skip next 2 dc, dc in Back Loop Only of next 6 dc *(Fig. 30),* (2 dc, ch 2, 2 dc) in next ch-2 sp, dc in Back Loop Only of next 6 dc, ★ skip next 4 dc, dc in Back Loop Only of next 6 dc, (2 dc, ch 2, 2 dc) in next ch-2 sp, dc in Back Loop Only of next 6 dc; repeat from ★ 3 times **more,** skip next 2 dc, dc in last dc (marked ch).

Repeat Row 2 for pattern until Throw measures approximately 47" (119.5 cm) from bottom point to top point *(Fig. 31)*.

Fig. 31

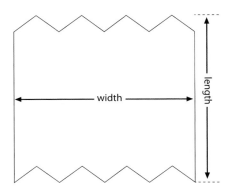

width

length

Finish off.

Weave in the yarn ends.

Yarn Information

The projects in this book were made using a variety of yarns. Any brand in the specified weight may be used. It is best to refer to the yardage/meters when determining how many skeins or balls to purchase. For your convenience, listed below are the yarns used to create our photography models.

COASTER
Lily® Sugar 'n Cream®
#01742 Hot Blue
#02316 Beach Ball Blue

SPA CLOTH
Lily® Sugar 'n Cream®
#00201 Jewels

SCARF
Lion Brand® Tweed Stripes®
#204 Caramel

COWL
Lion Brand® Heartland
#105 Glacier Bay

RIPPLE THROW
Lion Brand® Hometown USA®
#214 Virginia Beach
#201 Ocean

HAND MITTS
Patons® Classic Wool Worsted
#77404 Orchid

Instructions tested and photo models made by Janet Akins and Lee Ellis.

Production Team: Writer/Technical Editor - Cathy Hardy; Editorial Writer - Susan Frantz Wiles; Senior Graphic Artist - Lora Puls; Graphic Artist - Becca Snider Tally; Contributing Photo Stylist - Lori Wenger; and Contributing Photographer - Jason Masters.